Discipleship Books:

The Incarnation

By

Philip Watson

Dedication

Dedicated to my loving wife Dianne, and my three children, Andrew, Jonathon and Ruth.

My grateful thanks for allowing me to spend so much of my spare time writing these words.

Acknowledgments

My grateful thanks to Warren Portsmouth who patiently helped me review the manuscripts of my books. Warren suggested improvements and asked questions at appropriate points.

I also want to acknowledge the help of the Holy Spirit for inspiring me to write these books and for frequently reminding me of scriptures, relevant to topics, in each book.

This book is part of a quintet of books about Jesus. The other titles being:

> The Ministry of Jesus
> The Son
> He Changed Our World (Jesus' impact on six different people)
> Attitude In Jesus' Teachings (soon to be published)

Other books written by Philip Watson:

> Humility
> The Holy Spirit
> Great Summaries
> 80 Spiritual Principles

Books Coming Soon

1200 Great Quotes
Attitude In the Old Testament
Attitude In Acts, Epistles and Revelation
Evidence The Bible Is True
Creation or Evolution
The Father

Contents

Introduction..1

    Briefly, the debate in the early
    Church....................................6
    The Nicene Creed.........................6

In the Beginning...9

  Pre-incanation...10
  Incarnation..10

What I have planned, that will I do..............15

    The conversation at heaven's
    conference table..........................17
    God only wise.............................23
    Before he came he had the powers
    of a king.....................................26
    While on earth he became like a
    lamb..26
    At His death he was like a lamb. .26
    After His ascension he resumed
    the powers of a king....................26
    At his second coming he will not be
    meek like a lamb. Rather 27

Jesus' Role in the Plan.................................29

    Surrendering divine rights............34

Perfect Timing, Perfect Place.......................39

    Perfect Timing.............................42
    Perfect Way................................43

  The Review...85

The Purposes of the Incarnation..................95

  PURPOSE ONE – he came to
  communicate God's truth – direct from
  heaven..98

    HEAVEN..................................100

PURPOSE TWO – he came to show or demonstrate..............................105

PURPOSE THREE – He came to destroy the works of the devil..............................108

PURPOSE FOUR – He came to establish the Church..............................108

PURPOSE FIVE – He Came to save the world..111

What Does The Incarnation Mean To Us Today?..113

Love God...121

Appendix...123

The Nicene Creed..................................125

Introduction

It was nearly Christmas, and I was looking again at the models of the baby Jesus, Joseph, Mary, the shepherds, the animals and the wise men. For over 30 years in the Watson household, that is the way it has been. Every year, about the first of December, the Christmas tree, the lights, the tinsel - and the models of the baby Jesus, Mary, Joseph, the shepherds and the wise-men appear.

These models take pride of place on our mantle piece because my wife insists that we have the manger scene there each Christmas as a reminder 'Jesus is the reason for the season'.

For some reason, one December as I looked at those familiar models of the baby Jesus surrounded by his parents, the shepherds, the wise men and the animals, it dawned on me: both the amazing simplicity, and yet the amazing wisdom of God, to send his Son incarnate, as a human baby, into our World.

The word 'incarnate is not used outside of Christian circles, so it is important to try and define it's meaning. The prophet Isaiah summarized that definition with one single word, *Immanuel*, which means "God with us."

This book has been written to review the way Jesus came, and the reasons for his coming. Jesus could have been born into the family of the High Priest. Or into the family of King Herod. Or he could have been born in Rome, the center of the Empire. Or Jesus could have descended directly from heaven in great power and glory. Surely the latter would have been preferable to a baby, born in a manger in small town in a backwater of the Roman Empire, to a very ordinary young woman?

If Jesus had descended in great power and glory, surely even tyrant kings, like Herod, would have listened to him?

Instead of all these seemingly preferable options, Jesus was born in a manger in the small town of Bethlehem, to an ordinary mother.

In this book, I have attempted to explain why God choose this option over all the other options available. Why God chose to act subtly, instead of acting with great fan-fare.

Other options that God may have considered before sending Jesus were:

- Not sending Jesus at all, and simply writing his teachings on the clouds,so that the people of that time could look up to the clouds and seen the teachings of Jesus, and then written them down.
- Or God could have written Jesus' teachings on golden tablets and given them to angels to bring to the people of this Earth.

If God had chosen either option, it would not have been necessary to send Jesus as a human being, and would have avoided all the complications of Jesus coming incarnate into the world.

Instead of those two options, God chose to send his word via a real person, into a world of normal people ranging from:

- sinners to saints,
- the godly, and
- the godless.

Instead of words written on clouds or tablets, he sent his Word as a real person so that people of the time could touch and be touched, by God's word.

The option to send his Word to us as a real person was symbolized by the models that I viewed on our mantle piece, before writing this book.

Words on a cloud, words on golden tablets, Jesus coming as the son of the High Priest or as a son of the King would have all had their merits, but in wisdom were by-passed, and God's word came to us as a baby, born in a manger.

Some readers may be surprised to discover that this book is as much about the nature of God the Father, his love and wisdom, as it is about Jesus and the incarnation.

The essence of the incarnation is that Jesus was both fully God and fully human, at the same time. Fully human because he was born of the flesh, and fully God because he was born of God.

The Apostle John highlighted three significant

aspects of Jesus birth, at the beginning of his Gospel.

> "In the beginning was the Word, and the Word was with God, and the Word was God ... The Word became flesh and made his dwelling among us." John 1:1 & 1:14 (N.I.V.)

This dual nature is all part of the marvel of the incarnation.

The incarnation of Jesus is so important for Christianity that If I had a hand in determining how our Bibles were divided, it would not be divided into two as at present. Instead, there would be three divisions, named as:

- *Pre-incarnation* (Old Testament)
- *Incarnation* (Gospels)
- *Post-incarnation* (Epistles).

By the end of this book, I had come to two conclusions about the incarnation.

If we do not understand the incarnation, we do not understand the Christian faith! For at the center of the faith is Jesus – and the way he came and why he came, is the foundation the Christian faith is built on.

The incarnation is something to rejoice over, not just at Christmas, but every day of the year!

Briefly, the debate in the early Church

In the centuries after Jesus, a sect called Arians were part of the Christian Church. They claimed Jesus was essentially *a spirit being, who just happened to look like a real human.* In response to this, a number of conferences were called to sort out this issue. Was Jesus fully God or fully human or fully both?

One conference was held in the city of Nicea which is located in present day Turkey. The Christian leaders there discussed this question and at the end of the conference, wrote what came to be called the Nicene Creed.

That creed comes to using somewhat stilted language, but the Church leaders of the time came up with very exact words explaining how Jesus could be both God and human, at the same time.

The Nicene Creed

We believe in one God, the Father Almighty, maker of all things, both visible and invisible,

And in one Lord, Jesus Christ, the Son of God, Only begotten of the Father, that is to say, of the substance of the Father, God of God and light of light, very God of very God, begotten, not made, being of one substance with the Father,

By whom all things were made, both things in heaven and on earth,

Who, for us men and for our salvation, came down and was made flesh, was made man,

Suffered, and rose again on the third day, went up into the heavens,

And is to come again to judge both the quick and the dead,

And in the Holy Ghost.

The World Book Encyclopedia No 14, p198

The problem some people have trying to understand how Jesus could be both fully human and fully God at the same time is because they cannot understand, or believe, or conceive that God can move through multiple dimensions of space and time.

Chapter 1

In the Beginning

The first three words of John's Gospel and the first three words of the book of Genesis, are exactly the same i.e. "In the beginning..." That tells us that the Apostle John was making a significant point about Jesus, because he used exactly the same words at the beginning of his Gospel, as those found in the first book of the Bible – Genesis.

The first chapters of the book of Genesis are about the beginning of life, and of God's relationship of with the first human beings. Then as the first chapters unfold, there is the explanation of the reasons that this natural relationship was broken, and how it became more difficult for human beings to have a relationship with God, because of their sin.

The Gospels are about the beginning of a new era in world history, in which the dividing wall between God and humans beings would be demolished and a door opened into the throne room of God, Jesus being the doorway.

In the first chapter of his Gospel John made some key points which are the pillars of the doctrine of the incarnation.

Pre-incanation

> In the beginning was the Word
> ....the Word was with God,
> ....the Word was God. John1:1(N.I.V.)
> Through him all things were made...
> John1:3(N.I.V.)

Incarnation

> The Word became flesh and made his dwelling among us...John1:14(N.I.V.)
> In Him was life... John1:4(N.I.V.)

He was :

> "The true light," John1:9(N.I.V.)
> "full of grace and truth" John1:14 (N.I.V.)
> Able to give to those who believed in Him, "the right to become children of God." John1:12 (N.I.V.)

Other New Testament writers affirm what John wrote. The Apostle Paul wrote

- He was "in very nature God" Phil 2:6 (N.I.V.), and.

- "All of God's fullness dwells in him." Col 1:19.

The writer of the book of Hebrews wrote.

- He is "the radiance of God's glory and the exact representation of his being." Heb 1:3

Considering what John and Paul wrote about Jesus, it makes the birth of Jesus in a manger at Bethlehem, all the more remarkable.

Bethlehem had, according to Jewish records of the time, a population around one thousand people.

A British Broadcasting Corporation (BBC) documentary on the life of Jesus, offered insight into the type of place where Jesus was born. Excavations of the buildings in a nearby town, just south of Bethlehem, show that many houses had two stories.

An upper story where home owners and their families lived during the hotter summer months because it was cooler - and in the lower story during the winter months, where it was warmer.

The lower story was divided into two parts. The upper part where humans lived and the lowest level (about 1 yard lower), where the animals stayed out of the cold. Although the Greek word to describe that type of house *kataluna,* is frequently translated as "inn" (and we might picture the Bethlehem Hilton.) In fact a better translation of *kataluna* is upper level. So a more accurate picture of the place where Jesus was born, would be the lower level of the lower story – where the animals sheltered over-night. That is where, the *Son of God* was born!

The Son of God was not born in a palace, nor in something even remotely resembling a first century equivalent of the Bethlehem Hilton. So did God think that his Son should be born in these humble circumstances?

Undoubtedly, but that was only part of His master plan. God's attention to detail is significant, and evident in everything to do with Jesus' birth.

For the birth of Jesus was predicted to be to a normal 'human' birth by a virgin. If some think God went AWOL with the birth of his Son, a review of the details surrounding Jesus' birth show there was thought behind God's master plan.

From the world of matter, there was a bright star in the sky. From the heavenly realm, a host of angels. From the world of humans, there were both wise men and simple shepherds. At his birth were both male and female, young and old, and there were likely to have been guests on the upper level of various ages. And from the animal kingdom, donkeys, sheep and other domesticated animals.

So in God's plan, all the bases were covered. A variety of people, foreign dignatories, animals, angels, and a celestial light.

Any person in the town of Bethlehem who heard about the birth of Jesus, probably thought it was simply a case of, another little Jewish boy has been born to parents of no great significance, in a town of little importance. John noted that

> "He was in the world and though
> the world was made through him,
> the world did not recognize him."
> John 1:10 (N.I.V.)

And I imagine if we had been living at that time, most of us would have thought the same. That is unless we began to believe the stories associated with Jesus' birth.

Stories like:

- An army of angels appearing in the heavens.
- Angels visiting shepherds outside of Bethlehem.
- The visit of the angel Gabriel to Mary prior to her conception.
- Joseph's dream, and
- The arrival of the astrologers who recognized the significance of the star that shone so bright.

I wrote in the introduction that this book is as much about the nature of God the Father, his love and wisdom, as it is about Jesus and the incarnation, and in the next chapter, we will discover the detailed planning that preceded the birth of Jesus.

Chapter 2

What I have planned, that will I do.

Isa 46:11

In this chapter the spot light will be on God's role. In the Bible, the words "planned", "plans", and "plan" are frequently associated with God the Father. For example.

- "The things you planned for us....Pa 40:5

- But the plans of the Lord stand firm forever...Pa 33:11

- In him we were also chosen having been predestined according to the plan of him who works everything in conformity with the purpose of his will... Eph 3:11

If I held a poor opinion of God the Father it would be that the incarnation was ill-timed and ill conceived. Jesus was born in a back-water of the Roman empire, rather than in Rome, the capital. He was born two thousand years ago, rather than today when media could spread his fame around the world.

There are other aspects of his birth that almost make it look as if the incarnation lacked planning, and was a hasty decision made, to rescue the people of this earth!

Even though it may appear to some to have been an ill thought out and hasty, I believe that the real situation was the opposite of those insinuations.

- The planning had been in the pipeline for a long time. Isaiah who lived over 700 years before Jesus predicted his sufferings.

- Love was written all over those plans. John 3:16

- God's great wisdom can be seen so clearly in the 'how', 'when' and 'why' of the incarnation. There are multiple references in the Bible to the wisdom of God.

- The planning for the incarnation was done in 'consultation' with Jesus and the Holy Spirit.

Consultation? Already, some Bible scholars will be reviewing their knowledge of the Bible and asking "Where in the Bible does it say, the Father, Son and Holy Spirit, 'consulted' with each other, before Jesus came, incarnate into our world?"

The conversation at heaven's conference table

Said Eliphaz to Job. "Do you listen on God's council?"Job 15:8 (N.I.V.)

The English word council is translated from the Hebrew word *sod,* which means 'to consult'. The word signifies a friendly conversation among friends (Jer 6:11) or a serious consultation among Judges. Jer 23:18 The word *sod* is also used to denote a deliberation (Prov 15:22), a confidence (Prov 11:13), a familiar acquaintance. Job 19:19

So who are the members of God's council? There are only two beings we can be sure were at the council. The Son and the Holy Spirit – Matt 26:64 & 1 Cor 2:11. Possibly senior angels and/or the elders around the throne?

Aside from the debate about who was at the council, the word *sod* indicates consultation and deliberation takes place before any decision is made. Any planning done, is done in an atmosphere of friendly conversation and trust.

When Jesus said, "I and the Father are one" I believe that he meant one in nature, but also both of us are in total agreement about God's purposes.

Let us use a little imagination and imagine we were at the heavenly conference-table and able to listen in on the conversation between the three members of the trinity about the how and when Jesus would come to this earth.

The conference had been called to review God's relationship with his people and what could be done about it. The conversation may have gone like this.

NB Though I have used my own words in the following summary of the history of God's people,

it draws on summaries found in Acts chapter 7
(Stephen), Hosea chapter 4, Ezekiel 34: 1-6,
Daniel 9:6 – and similar references.

God speaking "Ever since Adam and Eve, I
have had trouble getting my people to listen to
me – but even when they do, sometimes they
listen and obey, while at other times they do
so only for a short time, then go their own
way. I have appreciated Noah, and Abraham
and Joseph and Moses, and David – people
who listened to my words and trusted me to
lead them. But there have been many others
who have scorned my advice and grieved me.

After I led my people out of Egypt with great
signs and wonders, within a short while they
were partying and worshiping a golden calf,
as if the golden calf had brought them out of
Egypt. Then after I had demonstrated my
great power and showed them I could part a
sea (the Red Sea), they still would not trust
me to help them defeat the people in the land
of Canaan. So I had to delay their arrival in
the land of Canaan for forty years.

Even when they got into the promised land,
sometimes they treated their fellow Israelites,
more like slaves, than citizens. After king
David, with rare exceptions such as
Jehoshaphat, the kings have ruled with only

their own comfort in mind.

At times, even the priests joined in taking advantage of foreigners, orphans and widows. The very people I wanted them to help."

There was a sigh at the heavenly conference table, and God paused before continuing. "We have raised up many different prophets to remind them of my ways and lead them back to the right way. Sometimes they have listened to the prophets. Other times they have imprisoned, killed or ignored them." Then God paused before asking this question. "Is it time I sent my Son - Jesus?"

The words, "Is it time I sent my Son?", are drawn from a parable Jesus told Matthew 21:31-45. In that parable, Jesus implied that God had finally had enough of sending prophets to his people, and had finally decided to send his Son as his ultimate representative.

We know that there was agreement at the heavenly conference table prior to his coming, because when Jesus came, he frequently used the words, "I have come...."

At the conference table they agreed on the broad outline of Jesus' coming but the question "how would Jesus arrive on the earth?" was the key focus.

One option they discussed was.

> "Jesus coming straight from heaven with great power and glory, so that the earthlings would be spell bound by his glory, and know for certain that he was the Son of God. And if he did come that way, the question was "Should he take with him, legions of angels (a legion numbers 5,120 to 6,000), as support."

There was further discussion about this option. The Holy Spirit asked. "Should Jesus have all the powers of heaven, available to him? For example, would he demonstrate divine authority by throwing himself off the highest point of the temple, and then onlookers would see, thousands of angels flying through the air to save him. Or turn stones into bread? Matt 4:1-7

Or any number of other demonstrations, that would prove beyond doubt, that He was none other than the Son of God!

Then a senior angel asked. "Wouldn't it be better if he was born as a normal human being, but born as a prince into the palace of one of the kings? Or born as a son of the High Priest or some other high-ranking religious teacher, such as a Pharisee or Sadducee?"

Other options may have been discussed.

"Should Jesus be born of a woman?" was a question asked at the heavenly conference table. If Jesus appeared out of nowhere, no one would know where he had come from, and he could begin his ministry without people saying he's just the son of a Torah teacher from Jerusalem. Or "just the son of a business couple from Bethlehem. " Or "just the son of a carpenter and his wife, from Nazareth" and dismiss the idea that he was the Son of God.

These options are likely to have been considered at the heavenly conference table.

- For Jesus to appear as a glorious King, direct from heaven
- For Jesus to be born as a Prince, or
- the son of one of the prominent religious leaders.
- Jesus just appearing in Galilee and starting his ministry, even though no-one knew who he was, nor where he had come from.

It seemed amazing to a senior angel present at the conference table that these three options were discarded in favor of an option that did not 'appear' to be wise. Jesus was to be born of a virgin, into an ordinary family, in a small town called Bethlehem. That was the plan they drew up, at the heavenly conference table.

God only wise

The Bible frequently speaks about the wisdom
of God. The Apostle Paul wrote in the book of
Ephesians about the "manifold wisdom of
God" 3:10, and in the book of Romans, Paul
exclaimed

> "Oh the depth of the riches of
> wisdom and knowledge of God!
> Rom 11:33 (NIV)

So how was God's wisdom applied to the
coming of Jesus, when there were many other
options, like those mentioned?

First of all we need to remind ourselves, that
the coming of Jesus was not a hasty decision
made at the last moment. The prophet Isaiah
who lived over 700 years before Jesus was
born, prophesied some of the key details
about Jesus' life in this well-known passage.

> Who has believed our message
> and to whom has the arm of the Lord
> been revealed?
> He was despised and rejected by
> men...
> But he was pierced for our
> transgressions.
> He was assigned a grave with the

wicked,
And with the rich in death,
Though he had done no violence
nor was any deceit in his mouth.
                    Isaiah 53:1-9 (abbrev)

The strategy selected would confuse many Jews because they could only think of the Messiah as someone more splendid and more powerful, than King David. At the heavenly conference table they discussed two strategies, the *lion* strategy and the *lamb* strategy. Would Jesus come like a lion or like a lamb?

If the lion strategy was the best option, then Jesus should come as a glorious powerful king, straight from heaven. If the lamb strategy was adopted, then he should come as a normal citizen. If he did come as a normal citizen, that meant he would be vulnerable to powerful people in the land.

After much discussion at the heavenly conference table, it was decided that 'both' options had advantages. Then a revolutionary idea was settled on. Jesus would come twice! The first time like a lamb, and the second time, like a lion!

We can see what it would have been like if the lion strategy had been adopted for the first coming of Jesus. In his own words.

> "They (all nations) will see the Son
> of Man coming on the clouds of the
> sky, with power and glory," Matt
> 24:30 (NIV)

The advantages and disadvantages of both
strategies are fleshed out in the chapter titled
Perfect Timing. Perfect place.

That Jesus was to come as a lamb was
prophesied by the prophet Isaiah.

> "... he was lead like a lamb to the
> slaughter ... " Isaiah 53:7 (NIV)

When Jesus' ministry on earth was about to
begin, John the Baptist was inspired to say
these words.

> "Look, the lamb of God who takes
> away the sin of the world." John
> 1:29 (NIV)

The contrast between the two comings, is
graphic. When Jesus first came as a lamb, he
was mocked, pushed from pillar to post by the
religious leaders, the Roman Governor, a
Jewish king and a crowd that had been incited
to ask for the release of a murderer.

Jesus' vulnerability to powerful leaders the
first time he came, will be a complete contrast

to the second time he comes. When he comes the second time as king of every king, every leader and every person will bow to Him.

The apostle Paul summarized the master plan in his letter to the Church at Philippi.

Before he came he had the powers of a king

"....Christ Jesus
Who, being in very nature God,
did not consider equality with God
something to be grasped,"

Phil 2:5 (NIV)

While on earth he became like a lamb

"....he had to be made like his brothers in every way..." Heb 2:17 (NIV)

At His death he was like a lamb

"he humbled himself and became obedient to death
-    even death on a cross." Phil 2:8 (NIV)

After His ascension he resumed the powers of a king

"Therefore God exalted him to the highest place and gave him the name that is above every name." Phil 2:9 (NIV)

At his second coming he will not be meek like a lamb. Rather ...

"... at the name of Jesus every knee should bow, and in heaven and on earth and under the earth, and every tongue confess that Jesus Christ is Lord ..." Phil 2:10-11 (NIV)

28   What I have planned, that will I do.

Chapter 3

Jesus' Role in the Plan

The pilot of a commercial airliner does not take to the skies with a plane-load of passengers and fly the plane where ever he or she likes. Rather, the pilot turns up at the airport at a time that is in 'sync' with the scheduling of the airline, and various organizations at the airport. The maintenance crew, the fuel handlers, cleaners, catering firms, and the air traffic controllers.

The pilot flies the plane to a specified destination, along a pre-defined route and at a predetermined altitude, as requested by the airline and approved or modified by air-traffic controllers.

Likewise when Jesus came, he did not just come when he felt like it, but came in sync with the Father's timing and many other factors that God had seen. This timing was in sync with where the Jewish nation was at. In sync with where the Roman empire was at – and undoubtedly other factors that we are not aware of.

The timing of Jesus coming was significant because the Roman empire was nearing its' zenith, when Jesus came to this earth. This factor was significant. Because the Roman Empire was near it's zenith, the Christian faith was able to spread like 'wildfire' throughout the Roman world.

Roman roads linked the empire and a multitude of peoples were connected by these roads. They were the greatest transport and communication devices this world had seen to that point. An empire which God had forseen.

So Jesus came, not only came in sync with the Fathers timing, but he came in sync with the Father's aims, and in sync with the Father's method.

The parable of the ungrateful servants is likely a summary of the thinking at heavens' conference table, before Jesus came to this earth. The words of that parable are.

> "Last of all, he sent his Son to them. They will respect my son ..."
> Matt 21:37 (NIV)

This was God's master plan. God had sent the prophets but finally he was sending his Son.

But what about Jesus' attitude? The word "sent" could imply two things. Either Jesus was told he was going to this Earth, and that was an order that had to be obeyed, implicitly. Or he could have come unwillingly and begrudgingly. Sometimes we do tasks that we have to do, but we do them grudgingly, to get them out of the way.

Is this the attitude Jesus came to this Earth with? He regarded it as a task he had do do, but did he do it begrudgingly? Or did Jesus come willingly because he 'wanted' to, and because he was 'in full agreement' with God's aims and purposes.

Jesus could have come with the attitude. 'I might as well go, and get this over and done with - this plan of my Fathers to save the wretched inhabitants of the earth from themselves – and once I have achieved the task. I'll be back in heaven as fast as I can, and my Father will be, off my back!'

That Jesus came voluntarily and willingly, is obvious from a number of statements he made. He taught the first disciples to pray in what is called 'the Lord's prayer.' In it are these words

> "... your will be done on earth, as it is in heaven." Matt 6:10 (NIV)

These words show that Jesus thought it was paramount to do God's will. Another time he said

> "My food," said Jesus, "is to do the will of him who sent me and to finish his work." John 4:34 (NIV)

These words of Jesus imply that doing God's will, was something that nourished him, and left him feeling, full and satisfied!

Apart from Jesus words, other verses in the Bible indicate that doing God's will, is entirely voluntary. Ironically, evidence for that comes from Satan and his cronies. Satan and a third of the angels walked out of heaven *when they felt like it* Jude 1.6. And the first two chapters of the book of Job tell us that Satan walked back into God's presence – *when he felt like it!*

From this example, we can conclude that Jesus, and any being in heaven, is given the freedom to obey God's will or oppose God's will: entirely freely!

That fact makes it all the more special the way Jesus came, and that he came at all. Jesus did not have to come. He did not *have* to become like us. He did not *have* to go through all the normal learning experiences of life.

Learning to walk, and normal child-hood experiences like being teased or bullied. Perhaps he was ridiculed with the words. "Come on Jesus, you are too religious." Or, Jesus you are clumsy, you missed the ball, you will never make the team."

The freedom Satan has means Jesus did not *have* to come and die for us. He came willingly, without any coercion. Jesus came because of his 'love relationship' with his heavenly Father. Jesus said, "As the Father has loved me..."John 15:9 (NIV).

To return to the heavenly council and the meaning of the Hebrew word *sod* signifies

> a friendly conversation among friends (Jer 6:11) or
> a serious consultation among Judges. (Jer 23:18)
> The word *sod* is also used to denote a

> deliberation (Prov 15:22),
> a confidence (Prov 11:13),
> a familiar acquaintance (Job 19:19.)

These various explanations of the meaning of *sod describe* the atmosphere at the heavenly council, during which Jesus decided to come to this earth, and fulfill God's plans and purposes.

Surrendering divine rights

The coming of Jesus voluntarily to this earth is all the more remarkable because implicit in the planning, Jesus was to shed the rights, authority and power he held in heaven.

The Apostle Paul summarized the way Jesus shed his heavenly privileges.

> "... he gave up his divine privileges...." Phil 2:5&6 NLT

Just before the start of his ministry, Satan decided to test Jesus on that point, testing him to see if he really had surrendered his divine rights. Satan came to Jesus with two tests, and he picked the right moment for these tests - just after Jesus had returned from a forty day fast.

NB Some commentators suggest that Jesus could not have done a forty day fast, but author and evangelist Mahesh Chavda wrote in his book *The Hidden power of prayer and fasting* that he regularly did forty day fasts.

At the time when Jesus was hungriest, Satan came to him and said in effect

> "Come on Jesus. You know you had enormous power in heaven to do virtually anything you wanted. Now that you are on earth and hungry, why not turn these stones into bread?"

Jesus rejected Satan's temptation by referring to the scriptures that says.

> "People do not live by bread alone, but by every word that comes from the mouth of God." Matt 4:4 (NLT)

So Satan tried another tack to see if Jesus really had forsaken the powers and privileges he held in heaven. This time Satan took Jesus to the highest point of the Temple and 'quoted the Scripture that said God will send his angels to prevent the Son of God from hurting himself. But Jesus firmly resisted that attempt, also.

That Jesus had voluntarily surrendered his divine rights, was again demonstrated in the Garden of Gethsemane, just before he was taken away for his trial and eventual crucifixion. There in the garden, when confronted by the High Priest and his guards,

Jesus said to his disciples

> "Do you think I cannot call on my
> Father, and he will at once put at
> my disposal, more than twelve
> legions of angels? Matt 26:53
> (NIV)

A legion had between 5,120 to 6000 men, so if Jesus had chosen to exercise his divine rights in the garden of Gethsemane, he could have called on between 61,440 and 72,000 angels. Not that the chief Priests and his soldiers could have resisted, even one angel.

Another factor for any mission to succeed, is the willingness to see it through. Some people will start a project with good intentions, but when problems arise or the project becomes delayed, they eventually give up.

When Jesus said to his disciples that his food was to do the will of him who sent me, he concluded these words with,

> "and to finish his work."John 4:34
> (NIV)

Jesus was so tempted to opt out of the idea of finishing his mission in the garden of Gethsemane that he sweated drops of blood. There he reminded himself he had come to Earth to accomplish God's will and he prayed these words.

"Yet not my will, but yours."

and with his last gasp on the cross, was,

"It is finished." John 19:30 (NIV)

All of the tasks he had agreed with the Father long before he came to this Earth, were now finished.

Chapter 4

Perfect Timing, Perfect
  Place

This chapter continues the questions raised in the introduction "Did the birth of Jesus in the small town of Bethlehem, instead of say, Jerusalem or Rome reflect the wisdom of God?" Was a stable the best place for the Son of God to be born?

If we had been at the heavenly council and chosen to advise God, we may have suggested that Jesus descend from heaven in great power and glory. That option will avoid all human involvement. This would mean no complications for Mary, such as possible divisions of opinion in Nazareth which will probably divide into four camps.

- Those who think Mary's child was the result of sexual intercourse with Joseph.
- Those who think Mary's child was the result of sexual intercourse with some other, unnamed man.
- Those who will believe Mary's story, that the conception is by the power of the Holy Spirit.
- Those who are not sure what to believe.

If Jesus descends directly from heaven, then there will be no whispers in town about the Mary's morality and mental state, and no debates about Joseph's integrity will occur.

If we were advising God, we may have suggested that it is better if Jesus is born into the family of the High Priest. Surely a better option than being born the step-son of a carpenter.

God had so many options, but chose the one we know so well – why?

In a previous chapter it was pointed out that the words "plans" and "planned", are associated with God the Father throughout the Bible - as are the words "wise" and "wisdom".

So we are left with the question. If God is so wise, and plans events well in advance, does the birth of Jesus in a stable in Bethlehem match what we know about the nature of God?

Apart from words, 'plans' and 'planned', 'wise' and 'wisdom', there is another word frequently associated with God the Father, throughout the Bible. It is the word, perfect. "Perfect knowledge", "the law of the Lord is perfect", "perfect faithfulness", "perfect peace". A number of times we find the phrase

> "his way is perfect". 2 Sam 22:31 &
> Pa 18:30.

By bringing these three ideas together, we get the idea that *God in his wisdom, planned the incarnation of Jesus, perfectly!*

Apart from wisdom being involved in God's perfect planning, we also know something else about His planning. The incarnation of Jesus was planned well in advance.

God let the prophet Isaiah know (who lived about 700 years before Jesus) that Jesus was coming as a servant king – one who would suffer. And God let the prophet Daniel know that Jesus was coming again as a glorious powerful king, about 2500 years before his second coming.

Of course we do not know when that will be, but what we can say is at that at least two and a half thousand years have already elapsed since the time of Daniel.

Perfect Timing

Jesus was born near the zenith of the Roman empire, arguably the greatest empire of all time. The Greek language 'Koine' was spoken throughout the Eastern part of that empire, making it easy for the first Christians to spread the new faith. And even though Latin was spoken in the Western part, Paul was comfortable with the idea that he could travel to Spain, in the Western part of the Empire.

That empire was to last over 400 years after the death and resurrection of Jesus, allowing the Christian faith to spread throughout the Roman world, and beyond. Though the Western part of that empire was eventually over-run, Christianity had by then become the main religion throughout the empire.

For approximately a thousand years, we know little about the expansion of Christianity beyond Europe, the Middle East and North Africa. By the time Europe emerged from the dark ages, Europe would become the greatest colonizing power on the earth.

As a result of that colonizing, Christianity has become the main religion in North America, South America, Australasia, and the Pacific. In significant parts of Africa and Asia, Christianity is strong as a result of European missionaries and traders.

So when Jesus was born some 2000 years ago, it may not have seemed the best time, but God could see the possibilities of the faith spreading, first of all, around the Roman empire, and then one day, throughout the entire world.

Perfect Way

It was while I was sitting silently in our lounge, viewing the models of the manger scene, that the inspiration came to write this book. I could see a scene so familiar to many readers. There was Mary and Joseph, the baby Jesus, the animals, the shepherds and the wise men.

But was there another way? What were the alternatives? One option was for Jesus to be born into the Royal house-hold of King Herod. This does not seem to be a good idea. Herod had two of his son's murdered out of fear they might usurp him and on hearing of Jesus' birth, Herod arranged for the babies of Bethlehem to be killed.

What about the family of the High Priest? From what we read about the High Priest of Jesus' time, that also does not appear to be a great idea as they were opposed to Jesus' ministry and teachings.

Finally, what about the option of Jesus descending from heaven in great power and glory, ready to tell all who would listen?

To illustrate that God's great wisdom and knowledge 'was' applied to the birth of Jesus as a baby in Bethlehem, I have created a 'fictional' scenario in which Jesus comes to earth in, glorious kingly power.

This fictional scenario has been created as a means to consider Jesus descending in glorious kingly power. A scenario that God is certain to have considered, then rejected in favor of Jesus being born as a baby in Bethlehem.

This fictional scenario draws on historical research I have done. For example, in the fictional scenario that follows, King Jesus, when he descends in great power and glory, stays in a palace in Jerusalem. Why a palace? It is not because I have a vivid imagination!

The reason Jesus is invited to stay in a palace

during his time on Earth is that excavations of the city of Jerusalem of that era have revealed King Herod had 'three' palaces in the city, and Caiaphas the High Priest, had one. So it is quite conceivable that if Jesus had come in kingly power, Herod would have been approached and asked if King Jesus could stay in one of his three palaces.

I am sure that such a request would have flattered to him. In the first (real) visit of Jesus, Mathew tells us that King Herod wanted to see this miracle worker.

Also in the fictional scenario you are about to read, Jesus is given tons of gifts. That may seem over the top, but I suggest is realistic, given that in that era of time, if you were going to visit a king or Queen, you brought gifts. For example, Joseph's brothers brought many gifts to him, because he was the second most powerful person in Egypt. When Queen Sheba visited King Solomon, he gave her 'tons' of gold as a gift. When the wise men came to see the baby Jesus, they bought gifts of gold, incense and myrrh.

In a few words, if you were going to have an audience with a king or queen in those times, you brought gifts. That fact is intertwined in the following fictional scenario, for it is certain that had Jesus come to this Earth in glorious kingly power, all those who came to see him would have brought gifts - tons of gifts.

This fictional scenario also explores the likely reaction of the people of the time, if Jesus had come to this earth in great power and glory – the first time.

JUDEA- at the time, Pontius Pilate was Governor – two months prior to the arrival of King Jesus

The Triumvirate

Pilate the Roman Governor and Caiaphas the High Priest were having one of their three monthly meetings to discuss matters of mutual interest. Meetings that in the opinion of both, helped clear the air of any misunderstandings that sometimes arose between the Roman authorities and the Jewish religious authorities. This meeting was well under way when, suddenly, a large glowing angel called Gabriel appeared in the room. Caiaphas, who was schooled in angels, immediately recognized him as an angel, and bowed to the floor.

Pilate, though not schooled in angels like Caiaphas, instantly recognized that this large being who glowed, must be some sort of god. Not only because he glowed, but also because he had some soldiers guarding the entry into this room, and they were under 'strict' orders not to allow anyone into the room, excepting an emergency. Obviously this glowing being had not entered through the doorway, but just appeared in front of them.

So despite not being schooled in angels, Pilate was soon face to the floor like Caiaphas, and trembling!

The angel Gabriel quickly addressed both Caiaphas and Pilate, saying "Please get up. I want to talk to you both. I have a very important announcement!"

Slowly, both raised their heads and, after seeing the reassurance in Gabriel's eyes, returned to their seats. When Gabriel saw that they were ready to listen he said. "In two months time, on the first day of the month of Nissan, when the sun dial indicates that it is mid-day, Jesus the Son of God is going to descend into the outer Temple courtyard." Then Gabriel paused to make sure that both were on board with what he had been saying, and then continued.

"He is going to stay for 21 days. During that time, he wants to meet with the members of the Sanhedrin (The ruling religious council). He would also like to meet a cross-section of the people of this country and perhaps visit one or two towns, outside of Jerusalem. He will bring with him some important teachings on gold tablets that God wants you (looking at Caiaphas), to teach the people!(pause) Do you have any questions?"

When Caiaphas finally found his voice, he said. "Does the Son of God, have any preferences where he would like to stay?" Caiaphas was already thinking about his palace as possible lodgings for king Jesus and then continued "I am happy to vacate my palace and let King Jesus stay there!"

Gabriel just smiled. "He does not need to stay in your palace. Any type of accommodation will be suitable."

Both Pilate and Caiaphas would later think of many other questions they wished they had asked Gabriel while he was still there, but they were too shocked by the sudden appearance of this mighty Arch Angel, to think clearly.

After the visit, both Caiaphas and Pilate forgot about the matters they had been discussing before Gabriel's visit, and began talking about, only one thing. 'The necessary arrangements for the visit of king Jesus - the Son of God!'

It was agreed that they and their representatives would need to meet three times a week (and more often if necessary) so that they could keep in touch on progress with their planning for the visit of King Jesus.

It was during the first meeting, they decided it would be best for King Jesus to stay in one of Herod's palaces, so they agreed that Herod's representatives should also be brought onto the organizing committee, effectively forming a triumvirate of planners. Caiaphas and his advisors, Herod and his advisors, and Pilate and his advisors.

What was quickly obvious to Pilate, though he was somewhat reluctant to do so, was that he would need to inform the Emperor sooner, rather than later.

All Roman Governors around the Empire were required to furnish at a minimum, weekly reports to the Emperor. Apart from these weekly reports, most Governors realized that the Emperor had their own 'sources' in each province, so that Pilate knew the Emperor would hear about the planning for King Jesus' visit, sooner or later, anyway.

What troubled Pilate, he did not know how the Emperor would react to his report of the visit by the angel Gabriel. Would the Emperor think that Pilate had lost his mind or ask? "Has he become insane? Or has he been drinking too much wine? Or has he become influenced by the religion of the Jews, or has he had some sort of religious experience?"

As it happened, when the Emperor got Pilate's letter, he considered all those possibilities and asked his attendants "Has Pilate become deluded or has he been drinking too much, or influenced by the religion of the Jews that he has sent me a letter claiming, a giant angel suddenly appeared at a meeting between himself and the High Priest.

Apparently this Angel told Pilate that the 'Son of God' will be descending from the sky into the Temple courtyard 7 weeks from now?" Soon after that, the Emperor sent urgent orders to his informants in Jerusalem to see if, in their opinion, any of these three scenarios were true.

It took about four days for messages to travel from Rome to Jerusalem (providing the seas were moderately calm) and at least another four or five days to receive a reply.

While the Emperor awaited a reply about Pilate's sudden insanity or binge drinking or religious experience, the Emperor mellowed in his opinion, deciding to cover both bases.

He decided that, in case Pilate had been telling the truth, he would like to meet this Son of God - the heavenly King. And if the 'Son of God' did not appear, he would remove Pilate from his position, in disgrace.

Either way, he would go to Jerusalem. In the Emperor's view it was worth taking the risk that Pilate was telling the truth about the visit of King Jesus. But in any case, reasoned the Emperor - a break from the politics of Rome would do him good.

What helped the Emperor begin to think that Pilate and Caiaphas had actually been visited by a large angel were the reports he got from his 'sources', in Jerusalem. None of them mentioned Pilate acting as if he was insane, drunk or deeply religious. The reports from his sources said, that both Caiaphas and Pilate looked, "very worried men and were continually busy, and that the lights in their residences were burning late into the night, every night."

The reports from the Emperor's sources stated that 'Pilate's and Caiaphas' assistants seemed to be hurrying here and there on endless urgent errands!' The Emperor's sources also told him that King Herod had suddenly come to Jerusalem, and taken up residence in one of his palaces. His sources also told him that Jerusalem was abuzz with rumors that the glorious Son of God would be coming soon!

After the emperor got these reports from his sources that Pilate was both sane and sober, though looking very harried by endless meetings, the Emperor ordered a dozen Tyremes (ocean-going ships) be made ready for his visit to Judea – and Jerusalem.

The date was fast approaching when King Jesus would come, so in the end the Emperor wrote to Pilate to say that he would arrive in time for the visit of King Jesus, and expected to he housed in "suitable" accommodation.

In that letter the Emperor also wrote "I will be there for the duration that King Jesus is in Jerusalem." In the same letter he asked Pilate to arrange several 'private meetings', with King Jesus.

Meanwhile in Jerusalem, when they were a third of the way through the 'endless' meetings, Pilate got the Emperor's letter informing him that he was coming to Jerusalem for the duration of King Jesus visit.

When Pilate opened the Emperor's letter, he threw his hands in the air exclaiming "This is the last thing I need. The emperor coming! Herod and Caiaphas and I are receiving daily requests from Kings in this part of the world, to come and visit Jerusalem during the period of King Jesus' visit. And now" he shouted "I have to house the Emperor and his retinue!"

After getting over his anguish that the Emperor was coming, Pilate wrote back requesting that the Emperor despatch legions from Egypt and Syria to Judea for the duration of the visit of King Jesus, and perhaps a third legion from elsewhere, to help maintain security, law and order.

For Pilate was well aware of many rumors already circulating about the visit of King Jesus, and it was likely tens of thousands of pilgrims were already making their way towards Jerusalem, along with brigands and other undesirables who may harry some of the pilgrims.

When the Emperor got Pilate's request for extra legions to be sent to Jerusalem, he agreed, though he wrote that the third legion should be kept in Galilee as standby, in case some stirred up trouble there. Only the legions from Syria and Egypt were to be in the precincts of Jerusalem, during the visit of King Jesus.

One of the letters the Emperor wrote to Pilate at this time, had a nasty twist. The Emperor made it clear in this letter that Pilate's reputation as a Governor was on the line and the Emperor, like others, was expecting to see when he got to Jerusalem; none other than 'The Son Of God' in all his glory. The nasty twist at the end of this letter, sent shivers down Pilate's spine.

The words were.

> "*If I find that Caiaphas and you were having some sort of delusional religious experience and that I have traveled half way across the Empire, only to find that my visit has been a waste of time, then two people will quickly find a home on a cross, outside of Jerusalem!*

Pilate knew exactly whom the Emperor was referring to, although he hoped the Emperor was wise enough not to crucify the High Priest.

What worried Pilate was not the truth that he

and Caiaphas had been visited by a large angel, but was 'What if King Jesus changes his mind or delays the visit for a while and the Emperor accuses me of being deluded.'

In the end, Pilate and Caiaphas and King Herod had too much to worry about to spend time considering whether King Jesus would change his mind.

There were interminable meetings. The angel Gabriel had said that King Jesus wanted to meet a cross-section of the community and the three power brokers had to make decisions about who, where and how.

One question was "Where would they arrange for a cross-section of the community to meet King Jesus?" It was decided after much debate that Jesus would meet them at a special dinner function at Pilate's headquarters. That did not please Caiaphas because though they could not say it explicitly, Jews were not supposed to dine with Gentiles.

Who was to be invited caused much debate between the three, and their representatives. Pilate knew enough about the Jewish religion not to suggest inviting immoral men and women to the dinner. He also knew enough about their values, not to suggest inviting

Samaritans to the dinner, but that left the door wide open for most others. Pilate was soon to learn that there were others the Jewish religious leaders did not want at the dinner, apart from sinners and Samaritans.

When they began to discuss 'who' should be invited from a cross-section of Judean society, Pilate kicked the ball off by suggesting that they invite several tax collectors, who had impressed the Roman authorities with the speed they had collected the full amount of taxes.

He thought it would be appropriate to reward at least two tax collectors, by sending them an invitation to the special dinner with King Jesus. Pilate said, "We could invite Matthew (later to become a disciple of Jesus) from Jerusalem, and Zaachaeus from Jericho to the dinner. They have done a fine job collecting taxes for our administration."

As soon as the word "tax collector" was mentioned, Caiaphas and his advisors half choked and tried not to blanch too awkwardly.

Even though they tried to disguise their reaction, Pilate picked up on it. He did not know that tax collectors were regarded by the religious leaders as being akin to immoral people and Samaritans. Quickly Caiaphas coughed and said something like. "I am sure that we can consider these two men but maybe there are others who would merit a place before these two um.... tax collectors?"

There were other groups, apart from tax collectors that the committee decided not to invite to the official 'meet King Jesus dinner'. It was felt that people from occupations like shepherds and fishermen and their families, were just "too low" - and too smelly, to meet King Jesus. In their discussions the committee then ranged onto other occupations that should not be invited.

People from the families of carpenters were another obvious group to exclude, though there was some discussion about carpenters. In the end it was felt that there were carpenters, and there were carpenters! The families of ordinary carpenters like those from the villages of Galilee (Nazareth/Bethlehem), should be excluded but the carpenters who made the fine furniture for King Herod's and Caiaphas's palaces, should be invited.

Finally the committee hammered out a list of people who would be 'acceptable' guests but there were many other decisions that had to be made about the visit, which ended in the lap of one of the three power brokers.

Each power broker ended up being given some primary tasks. Pilate's responsibility was security. Herod's was accommodation, and Caiaphas was responsible King Jesus' itinerary

What irritated Caiaphas was the way the other two power brokers made frequent suggestions about what King Jesus should do and should not do, during his spare time. They were forgetting that Jesus was not a human King, but the Son of God.

By this time Pilate got the Emperors letter stating he was coming, Pilate was all too aware that many other World leaders had suddenly decided to visit Jerusalem during the month of Nissan, and he would need to ensure they were kept safe as well. For Pilate, this caused sleepless nights as he began to worry about the security and adequacy of accommodation for the Emperor, King Jesus, and all these other rulers.

Herod for his part, though flattered by the thought of playing host to so many kings and Queens, soon assessed he had a problem. Where to accommodate them? He had 'only' three palaces in Jerusalem. One had been assigned to King Jesus. One to the Emperor and one for himself. He was happy to have at least one other king or queen and their entourages stay with him in the guest rooms in his palace, but what of all the other kings, queens and rulers, who were arriving?

What made the problem even greater, was that this was a last minute thing! These rulers had heard that King Jesus was coming on the first day of the month of Nissen, and because time was short, they had more or less set out on their way towards Jerusalem straight away, sending letters ahead to tell Herod they were coming - never thinking that most other rulers in that part of the World were doing the same.

Herod's problem was simple. He did not have the capacity to accommodate these rulers – at least not in the style they were used to.

So three weeks before the arrival of King Jesus, Herod exclaimed at one of the meetings with the other two power brokers "We have all these rulers coming from all over the Empire. Twelve so far! Do they think I have twelve palaces in Jerusalem to accommodate them? I have Eugenie from Syria, Queen Candace from Ethiopia, Queen Cleopatra from Egypt and .... "

Then he stopped mid-sentence and said, cryptically "I had better keep those two women apart or there will be trouble" for

Herod knew that these neighboring countries had fought each other, many times over the years. After that comment, Herod looked at the other two, and waved his hand saying "So where can I accommodate them?" Meaning, the rulers!

Although Caiaphas and Pilate had left accommodation in Herod's lap, they also felt partly responsible. They did not want unhappy rulers on their doorsteps complaining and arguing over the inferior accommodation they had been given, compared to other Kings or Queens.

It was a problem none of the three wanted. Their focus was the comfort of King Jesus and the Emperor – and ensuring that all the arranged events went smoothly.

In the end, they felt they had no choice but to make an unpopular decision. They drew up a list of fifteen (fifteen: to allow for any rulers who insisted on coming at the last moment) wealthy Jerusalemites and sent them a letter in which they wrote:

We know that you will regard it an 'honor' to have King and Queen .... stay at your house during the month of Nissen and know you will understand that this is a situation that has been imposed on us by the circumstances of the visit of King Jesus! So that we can make the appropriate security arrangements for their stay, we require you and your family to 'vacate' your homes within two days of the receipt of this letter. We will place guards around your home after you vacate it. Please leave all your furniture and fittings.

Signed. Herod, Pilate and Caiaphas

Apart from security for the Emperor and rulers and King Jesus, other security issues began to surface. Word had quickly spread about the coming visit of King Jesus, and already pilgrims were streaming towards Jerusalem to stay with relatives, or in any accommodation available.

Already petty thieving had begun to trouble pilgrims as they made their way towards Jerusalem, with their gifts.

One group who were initially *very* excited by the talk of the Messiah, the Son of God coming, were the zealots. They were known to be zealous for God, so zealous that they out-did the Pharisees in observing the law. Further, they were zealous that Israel only have 'one God', and the occupying Roman legions represented to them, Roman gods. So a zealot felt he was doing God a favor by murdering a lone Roman soldier, or one of their Jewish lackeys.

Pilate, as he racked his brain over the various security problems, soon found that his thoughts came to a halt whenever he thought about the zealots. Would they rejoice at the coming of the Son of God and just be happy?

Or would they use the time when King Jesus was in Jerusalem, a time when there would be perhaps millions of Jews in and around the city, as an opportunity to encourage the Jews to rise up and rid the country of the godless Roman occupiers?

That last thought troubled Pilate greatly. Millions of Jews incited by the zealots and so he came to one of the meetings of the triumvirate with this proposal.

"All the zealots should be rounded up during early morning raids and given an *involuntary* holiday, at a special camp set up near Damascus under the supervision of the spare legion that the Emperor had ordered to the region."

The other two parties agreed with Pilate and soon after that during dawn raids, most of the known zealots were arrested and taken in chains to their holding pens, near Damascus.

Caiaphas and Herod also wanted to be rid of the Romans, but not as a result of a zealot-led uprising and not at the time of the visit of King Jesus, so they agreed to Pilate's proposal.

As for the zealots, a few escaped the drag-net operation because of luck. One of them, who was simply known to his neighbors as 'Simon the zealot', was staying with an uncle in Bethany when the early morning raids took place, so he was not at home.

Simon soon heard about what happened, and after that, made a point of lying low - and out of sight until King Jesus returned to heaven. For the next month or so, if Simon did go out, he ventured disguised as a visiting Parthian Jew.

The angel Gabriel had requested that King Jesus visit several towns outside of Jerusalem, which caused debate among the committee members. The choice of which towns to select was made more difficult because once word got out that King Jesus wanted to visit several towns, delegations led by local mayors began to approach the triumvirate committee, asking that their town be considered as one of the two King Jesus would visit.

The dignitaries from most towns were to

return disappointed. They were not given any specific reasons why their towns were not selected. But the committee members knew, and notes were made about why various towns were rejected as being unsuitable.

> Bethlehem – *Too small*
> Bethany – *Too near Jerusalem*
> Emmaus – *Nothing to commend it*
> Cana – *In Galilee**
> Nazareth – *in Galilee **
> Tiberius (on the shores of lake Galilee) – *Could be affected by storms*
> ** Jews from Jerusalem, regarded Galileans as second class Jews.*

In the end, Caesarea (named after the Caesar) on the coast, was one of the towns selected. Caesarea was Pilate's choice, and Jericho in the Jordan valley was Herod's choice. Caesarea was an obvious choice for Pilate. It had an amphitheater in it and he envisaged they would hold a variety of athletic events, including both boxing and wrestling, for King Jesus to see.

Jericho was selected by Herod because of the hot springs and indoor baths which Herod liked. He was also partial to the wines produced around Jericho which had a special flavor because the vines were fed by local spring water. Added to that, there were attractive palms that grew within the town and along the roads nearby.

Pilate liked the choice of both towns because he knew they were easy to isolate from unwanted persons.

That was the way the triumvirate worked. On some points, Pilate and his advisors won. On others, Herod and his advisors won, and Caiaphas and his advisors on yet other points.

Because the crucifixion of most Jews was distasteful to Caiaphas and the high Priests, they sought agreement from Pilate that there be no crucifixions during the time King Jesus was in town. They spoke with mock sincerity.

> "With respect Governor, during this time of celebration when the *Son of God* is here, we would prefer that he not see anything as distasteful as a man hanging bleeding on a cross! Could it be that during his visit all crucifixions will be suspended?"

Pilate needed little persuasion on this point and added this request to the list of orders he had issued for the duration of King Jesus' visit. Some of those orders are listed below.

ORDER no 8: All beggars are to be removed from the streets of Jericho and Caesarea during the visits of King Jesus. There were blind beggars (such as Bartimaeus) near towns like Jericho, and the triumvirate did not want King Jesus to see beggars calling out as he passed by.

ORDER no 9: All zealots are to be rounded up during early morning raids and taken in chains to a holding camp near Damascus. There they will be guarded by companies from the 9th legion, until King Jesus has ascended.

ORDER no 13: All crucifixions are to be suspended immediately, until after King Jesus leaves this earth.

Preparations for the Visit?

For members of the Sanhedrin and their wives, the visit of King Jesus was a very exciting time! They ordered new dresses and cloaks because they had been invited to one of the official banquets. Both the members of the Sanhedrin and their wives, debated at length over what type of material and colors would be suitable.

White to reflect purity? Gold to reflect kingship? They asked themselves "Would it be appropriate to wear colorful dresses and scarves?" The husbands, being members of the Sanhedrin, had formal attire they were expected to wear but for the wives, there was no norm to go by.

For other groups in and around Jerusalem, it was also an exciting time. Many businesses found that orders were 'going through the roof' in the period up to and including the visit of King Jesus.

Those who sold material to make dresses and gowns, soon sold out of their stock and rapidly ordered in more - and yet more again. The craftsmen who produced gifts, soon found that their supplies vanished out the door, and they like other traders of similar goods were able to command top prices!

Those who sold food or drink of any kind, soon sold their stocks and were urged to get more. Anyone who sold grain or fowls or lambs or herbs, spices or figs or dates or fruit or wine (and other foods eaten at banquets), soon found that their stocks were exhausted, and placed urgent orders for more.

Very quickly the word went out among traders "If you want to sell food of any kind in the near future, Jerusalem is the place to be!" At that time, the traders grapevine hummed "There will be millions of hungry pilgrims heading towards Jerusalem! Hungry legions, rulers from neighboring states, not forgetting the

"Emperor and his retinue."

These rulers were not the types who liked to be seen dining off bread and water. It was imperative they have, ample supplies of the best food.

Many shepherds in near-by countries such as Syria, Jordan and Saudi Arabia, decided to drive their flocks to Jerusalem, and make a once-in-a-life-time killing by selling their flocks at top prices, and as a bonus staying on to see the Son of God before returning home again.

In towns like Nazareth, the word spread quickly that "The Messiah, the Son of God would be descending into the Temple courtyard on the first day of the month of Nissen." There was hardly any other topic people talked about.

In Nazareth, a young engaged couple called Mary and Joseph also talked about this amazing news. Mary spoke with Joseph.

Mary: "I dreamed that King Jesus would stop and talk with me."

Joseph: (being a more practical carpenter) "Mary, I don't think the High Priest's guards will let you get near King Jesus."

Mary: "I have been talking with Sarah and virtually the whole town in going to Jerusalem while the Messiah - King Jesus is there."

Joseph: "I have heard the same. Rachel is staying in town here to look after her mother who is too old to travel and I have heard that Jeconobab does not want to leave his business in case someone tries to break in and steal his equipment. But apart from those three, virtually everyone else, is going!"

Mary: "I have heard Uncle Laban, who makes furniture for Herod's palace, and Aunt Elizabeth have been invited to a special dinner to meet King Jesus, and they are so excited! Do you think it is possible you will get an invitation?"

Joseph: "I have been talking with some of my customers, and they have noticed that those who received invitations to these special dinners, are from select occupations. With few exceptions, none are from Galilee! You know how they (the people of Jerusalem) look down on us who live in Galilee."

Mary: "Are you and your family going?"

Joseph: "Yes. I and all my family are going to Jerusalem for about 2 weeks. We don't know where we will stay. We have friends there, but they say they will be overflowing with relatives, so if necessary we will just have to camp on the hillsides outside Jerusalem.

I will lock up my business and I have asked Jeconobab to keep an eye on it, but I suspect he is going to be too busy watching his own business to worry about mine. I've committed my house and business into God's hands. If I lose my tools to thieves, so be it. I am not going to miss this chance to see the Messiah."

Mary: "My family and I are going too. We are going to stay at Aunt Elizabeth's house while King Jesus is in the city. So even if it is unlikely I will get a chance to talk to King Jesus, Uncle Laban and Aunt Elizabeth will tell us all about the dinner with him, and we will ask them what King Jesus said, and what he looks like."

Joseph: "If you tell me where your Aunt and Uncle live, I will come and visit you there on the days King Jesus goes to visit Jericho. I hear he is going to visit Caesarea."

The Descent In Glory

When the visit finally came, those waiting in the vast Temple courtyard (estimated to cover about twelve football fields) were a mixture of religious and secular dignitaries, their wives and mistresses. Also waiting in the Temple courtyard were the trumpeters and Temple musicians.

Outside of the Temple courtyard and forming a column either side of the route that the procession would travel towards one of Herod's palaces, were members of the Tenth legion that had been brought to the city.

The soldier's uniforms were spic and span. Their armor was gleaming, the leather parts of their uniforms polished with oil. On specially erected stands were the legions trumpeters, ready to blow their trumpets in a fanfare as soon as King Jesus emerged from the Temple courtyard.

The legions standards were displayed prominently for all to see – much to the disgust of religious Jews who considered these standards as symbols of a godless power. Under the law of Moses, images were prohibited, and so the flags and symbols of the Tenth legion caused angst.

Packed on the roofs of houses and the walls of Jerusalem were the rest of the population and some of the many visitors to the city. Outside of the city on the surrounding hills, people crowded on the higher parts where the best view could be obtained of the Temple courtyard.

On the Mount of Olives, which overlooks the city, people could not move. Some estimated there were two to three million people in and around Jerusalem on the day King Jesus descended from heaven.

When King Jesus appeared in the clouds, those waiting, were not disappointed. First of all, two mighty angels appeared in the heavens, blowing their trumpets. Then King Jesus appeared between them, glorious in his splendor, accompanied by hundreds of angels singing praises to God. While they sang, King Jesus descended majestically, into the outer courtyard of the Temple.

The Kings, Queens, rulers, military commanders, Priests, members of the Sanhedrin and their wives, who were used to people bowing before them, when they saw the glorious King Jesus descending, did not hesitate to bow quickly to the pavement and kiss it reverently.

These religious leaders and rulers, scarcely dared to look at him, for they had never seen anything like it before. There was no doubt in their minds, that he was the Son of God!

The sight of King Jesus descending in his glory accompanied by hundreds of angels, produced a similar reaction among those watching from the walls of the city and other vantage points. For a few seconds they watched in awe, then, as if triggered by some automatic switch, quickly bowed their heads to the ground, not daring to even look at him.

When King Jesus finally landed in the Temple courtyard, and seeing everyone in the courtyard prostrate, he went to Caiaphas tapped him on the shoulder and said "Arise." Very slowly, Caiaphas rose to his feet. Taking their cue from Caiaphas, the other religious, civil and military leaders also arose.

Lost for words and embarrassed by the silence, Caiaphas turned towards the Temple musicians and trumpeters and indicated by a wave of his hand that they should now begin playing the music they had been rehearsing.

Events moved on quickly, and King Jesus began to work his way through the official program, of which, only some events are recorded in this scenario.

One day along with the Chief Priests, Jesus visited the Temple courtyard. While there, Jesus talked to the traders selling lambs and doves to people who came for purification ceremonies, dedications or consecrations – as demanded by the law. He also talked to the money changers and took an interest in the exchange rate they charged for Jews who came from most parts of the Roman Empire.

King Jesus expressed surprise at the prices they charged, then he began to ask some uncomfortable questions. "Do pilgrims have to buy their lambs and doves here, or can they buy them elsewhere?" One of the traders quickly replied. "No your majesty, pilgrims can only buy their animals here."

There was a quick flash of anger on Jesus face as he moved on. He began to suspect it was a monopoly system that forced worshipers to pay the higher prices.

On other days, Jesus went along with the official program of dinners with a selected cross-section of the community. No Samaritans, tax collectors, sinners or people from common occupations like shepherds, fishermen and carpenters were at these dinners.

On other days, there were state banquets with world leaders, special services in the Temple and visits to the two towns, designated for visits.

On the day that King Jesus and the official party traveled down the steep road towards Jericho, Jesus noticed the glint of sun on the armor of Roman soldiers, stationed about a quarter mile back from the road, on both sides.

These soldiers were standing ten yards apart. When he saw them, King Jesus stopped the official entourage, and asked the reason for the numerous soldiers. He was told that from time to time, travelers on this road are robbed by thieves.

King Jesus smiled and said. "Do you not think that I could call on twelve legions of angels to protect me, if needed?" Cf Matt 26:53 King Jesus was irritated by the overt security wherever he went, but this was the first time he began to let his irritation be known.

In both Jericho and Caesarea the walls of the houses in the towns received fresh coats of paint in compliance with the committee's order. The blind and any other beggars who normally lined the streets of Jericho were removed and taken to a nearby town during the time of King Jesus visit. The authorities did not wish King Jesus see the likes of people like blind Bartimaeus, * as he passed

by. *C.f.Mark10: 46-52

During his visit to Jericho King Jesus noticed a vendor on a side-street selling doves, so he stopped the entourage and asked the man the price he charged. The man told King Jesus the price, thinking Jesus wanted to buy some. He offered Jesus some doves for free. King Jesus thanked him for the offer, but declined.

Before he left the vendor of doves, Jesus commented. "The price you charge here is a lot cheaper than the price they charge for doves in the Temple courtyard! "The man, somewhat embarrassed said "Oh well, that's Temple prices for you and the Temple authorities take their cut too! "A glare from one of the Priests in the official party, quickly ended that conversation.

The trip to Caesarea on the coast, was notable for several incidents. Soon after King Jesus and the escorting party of Roman troops, Pilate, Caiaphas and some senior Priests, had left Jerusalem to travel down to Caesarea, Jesus asked the official party to stop. He had noticed well over a hundred large tents on the hill-sides near Jerusalem, and none of the pilgrims camping nearby were allowed near these tents. The tents were guarded by hundreds of Roman soldiers.

When the official party stopped, King Jesus

asked Caiaphas, "what are those tents for?" Because it was not his responsibility, Caiaphas looked towards the most senior military officer present to answer that question. When a legionnaire came over and heard King Jesus repeat the question, he said. "Those tents your majesty, house the gifts that the millions of pilgrims have brought with them.

Each person and each family who has come to see you wanted to give their gift to you personally. But with millions wanting to do that, my soldiers have had to tell them. "We will take your gifts, store them securely in our tents, and make sure that King Jesus sees them."

"As you will appreciate, we have already filled all the spare warehouses in Jerusalem with gifts from the Emperor and other world rulers, so these gifts from the millions of pilgrims are now in the tents that you see." Then the Centurion paused, before resuming. "Perhaps your majesty could advise us what you want done with these gifts?"

Jesus grimaced, when he heard the legionnaire tell him this, for he had seen inside some of the warehouses in Jerusalem full of large gifts that world rulers and members of the Sanhedrin had given him.

The visit to Caesarea was little different from the visit to Jericho. The only thing that was canceled from the official program at King Jesus 'emphatic' insistence was a fight to the death between two condemned criminals. It was during the visit to Caesarea that Jesus asked more uncomfortable questions of his hosts. "Where are the children" he asked? He had seen a few peeking from behind doors as his official party swept by, but he realized that they had been kept out of the way and were nowhere to be seen in any of the arranged banquets and functions. So Jesus said to Caiaphas "During the next function I want to meet children and I want to spend time with them."

King Jesus had come with scrolls that contained his teachings and at the dinners and banquets with the Sanhedrin and world leaders, he used those occasions to instruct them. During one of the banquets with the members of the Sanhedrin, many wanted to ask King Jesus questions, but were not allowed to.

Among questions they wanted to ask were "Which are the most important commandments?" and "What must I do to inherit eternal life?" A Pharisee called Nicodemus tried to arrange a private meeting with King Jesus to ask these questions, but that request was quickly rebuffed by Caiaphas and the committee.

At one banquet, King Jesus told the religious leaders that two commandments were the most important of all. "To love God with all your heart mind, soul and strength" and the second was one they had never heard of before. "To love your neighbor, as yourself". Because they had never heard of this commandment, Caiaphas politely asked King Jesus to clarify who is my neighbor for as Caiaphas explained. "Our law prescribes the ways in which we can help our fellow Jews."

Jesus replied "Your neighbor is everyone! Even a man or woman who has led an immoral life. A tax collector, a Samaritan! God loves those people too - equally."

Caiaphas blanched when he heard King Jesus use the words "immoral", "Samaritan" and "tax collector", for they were amongst the groups of people he and his fellow religious leaders avoid like the plague and considered to be good for only one place - Hell.

Jesus continued. "In fact that is why I have come. To call 'all' people, even sinful people to enter the kingdom of God. After those comments, Caiaphas drew the banquet to a close and thanked King Jesus for his "enlightened" teachings.

Towards the end of King Jesus' visit, he began to ignore the official program and one day went out onto the hillsides outside of Jerusalem, and taught the people. He healed many, freed some who were possessed by demons, and picked up children to bless them.

On the second to last day, King Jesus greatly disturbed the authorities by taking a whip into the Temple courtyard, and drove out the money changers and those selling doves for sacrifice, saying:

> "It is written in the Scriptures that my Temple will be called a house of prayer. But you are making it a hideout for thieves." Cf Matt 21:13 (G.N)

> "I have been to Jericho, and know the prices they are charging for doves there. Here in the Temple, you are charging four times that price!"

By the time King Jesus was ready to return to Heaven, the Emperor and some of the world leaders had already left Jerusalem. The Emperor citing illness.

The Emperor was originally scheduled to have two private meetings with King Jesus but canceled the second. He sent an apologetic letter saying he was feeling unwell. An aide of the Emperor quipped privately. "It's 'truth sickness' the Emperor has got a large dose of." When the Emperor had his first meeting with King Jesus, King Jesus continually said to the Emperor, 'I tell you the truth....''

Most other world leaders were the same. Once they had heard King Jesus' teachings, decided they had other things to do with their time while in Jerusalem, some quietly slipping out of the city citing reasons like "Important issues have arisen, at home."

Some of the teachings King Jesus gave at the banquets, did not appeal to them at all. Among those teachings, were:

> Blessed are the poor in spirit, for theirs is the kingdom of heaven...
> Blessed are the meek....
> Blessed are those who hunger and thirst for righteousness....
> Blessed are the merciful...
> Blessed are the pure in heart...
> Blessed are the peacemakers.....

King Jesus also taught people to

> Forgive your enemies....

In the thinking of the rulers, there was only one thing you did with your enemies. It was not a matter of 'if' they would be killed, but how. So King Jesus' teaching about forgiving their enemies did not fit in with their ideas. Most leaders quietly left Jerusalem, but not all.

Queen Candace of Ethiopia requested a private session with King Jesus and she was slotted into the private meeting the Emperor canceled. She was passionate about taking King Jesus' teachings back to Ethiopia.

As for the teachers of the law, one observed "Instead of supporting what we teach, many of King Jesus' teachings are contrary to them. His teachings have a lot to do with 'attitudes'. His teachings focus on attitudes to prayer and attitudes to fasting and attitudes to giving and righteousness. We do those things publicly so others can see that we are doing them."

He continued "Surely that is what is important? And surely God does not care for Samaritans, the immoral and tax collectors? We teach that people are either in, or out of God's favor, and these people are definitely out! Does King Jesus really believe that God loves these people, too!"

To their credit, not every teacher of the law dismissed Jesus' teachings. Some of the them were drawn to what Jesus was saying. People such as Nicodemus and Gamaliel (John 3:1-2 & Acts 5:34). They began to suggest to the members of the Sanhedrin that perhaps their teachings had gone down the wrong path.

The religious teachers were focussed on observing each of the hundreds of laws and being 'seen' to do the right thing. Whereas King Jesus addressed their attitudes to doing the right thing, such as showing mercy to sinners.

As for the millions of pilgrims who came from every part of the empire, many never saw King Jesus. Just over half saw him briefly as he traveled with the official party to and from Jericho and Caesarea. That is all Joseph, a carpenter from Nazareth, saw of King Jesus.

About 1 in 5 of those who had crowded into Jerusalem before the Roman authorities closed the city off, saw King Jesus going to and from the official banquets and meetings with world leaders. Mary from Nazareth came within four yards of King Jesus several times as his entourage passed by. Each time she felt a glow in her spirit as he passed by. One time, King Jesus looked directly at her, and smiled.

Joseph also saw King Jesus along with about 150,000 others on the day King Jesus spent among the crowds on the hillsides outside of Jerusalem - teaching them, healing some, and setting free any who had demons in them.

In the end when King Jesus ascended into the heavens, most were sad to see him go, but others, glad. After he left, Caiaphas and the chief Priests did not know what to do with the tablets containing His teachings, for they had expected King Jesus would whole-heartedly support their religious teachings, life-style and theology.

However, it seemed to Caiaphas and the chief Priests that King Jesus questioned most of their teachings, practices, life-style and theology. Then he had the audacity to introduce many new teachings.

Caiaphas and the teachers of the law felt these teachings of King Jesus were dangerous if people with unstable minds were able to read them, and worse, believe them. So after King Jesus returned to heaven they announced that his teachings were being stored in the Temple treasury for *safe-keeping* and at 'suitable' times, these teachings would be brought out. They did not specify what were suitable times.

The Review

According to what we know of Scripture, the heavenly council planned that Jesus would come the first time as a servant-king, and the second time as, the "king of Kings". You have just read what it may have been like if Jesus had come the first time as a glorious, heavenly King. I.e. The lion strategy.

Now it is time to give credit to God. It is certain that He, and the members of the heavenly council, had thought through the scenario you have just read. They knew about the palaces Herod had. The knew about the expectation of that time, that if a person came before a king, they were required to bring gifts. And the more significant the king was, the greater the number and the greater the value of the gifts expected.

It is certain that God the Father and the heavenly council knew that King Jesus would be treated to banquets and functions, to whom only appropriate and vetted persons were invited.

They anticipated that if King Jesus came in great power and glory, he would be closeted in a palace and confined to official services and functions and banquets.

We also have to assume that the heavenly council considered every other scenario. Such as:

- Words written on the clouds. Some people of the time would have written these words down and stored them away, and there would be a small sect who followed these teachings.

- Angels bringing golden tablets containing Jesus' teachings which probably would have been locked away in the Temple.

- Born into King Herod's family. (Probably Jesus would have been executed as a threat to King Herod's reign, like two of his other sons)

- Born into the family of the High Priest. (Probably Jesus would have been arrested for heresy before his ministry began)

We have to believe that these scenarios were considered, but God in his great wisdom rejected these options before deciding that the best way for Jesus to come was:

> Born to a virgin named Mary, and raised in a town called Nazareth. Because of that, he was free to move wherever he liked, and talk with whoever would listen. He was free to call to be his disciples, anyone he chose. He called a tax collector named Matthew, and a zealot named Simon to become disciples, and fishermen.

The heavenly council foresaw it was better that Jesus' teachings were written first of all on the hearts and minds of his disciples, and only later on paper.   Rather than angels bringing tablets containing his teachings being locked away in the Temple Treasury.

In the heavenly council, it was planned that Jesus should be a free agent, able to travel where he wanted. Galilee was at the 'heart' of his ministry on Earth while in the Kingly scenario you have just read, Jesus never went to Galilee because Galilean Jews were regarded as second-class citizens by those in Jerusalem.

In the Gospel accounts, Jesus was raised in the home of a carpenter from Nazareth. In the kingly scenario, Nazareth and the homes of a carpenters were regarded as too basic and too low-cast to be considered worthy of a chance of meeting King Jesus.

In the real ministry of Jesus, he was able to pick up children and bless them. If he had come as a glorious king it is likely they would not have got near him. We do not know for sure, but during Jesus' real ministry it is believed he lived in a house in Galilee. Some speculate it was Peter's house. Whether it was Peter's house or not, is conjecture.

Regardless of whose house it was, it is likely that there were children there, and Jesus may have played with them in the evenings.

In the real ministry of Jesus, he had a tax collector, a zealot and fisherman among his disciples. In the scenario you have just read, such people would not have got near him. Zealots like Simon were rounded up (or had to go into hiding).

In the real ministry of Jesus, Matthew, a tax collector, was called to be a disciple and Jesus invited himself to the home of another tax collector called, Zaachaeus. In the kingly scenario, tax collectors would not have got near Jesus.

In the real ministry of Jesus, he stopped to heal blind Bartimaeus who called out from the roadside when Jesus passed through the town of Jericho. In the kingly scenario, lepers, the blind and all who begged were cleared from the roadsides of the two towns he visited so that King Jesus would not even see them.

In the real ministry of Jesus, he spoke with Samaritans and immoral women and healed those with leprosy. In the kingly scenario, people like that would never not have got near him.

In the real ministry of Jesus, a woman with an incurable disease was able to reach out and touch him. Mary Magdalene was able to pour expensive perfume on his feet. John was able to lean on his chest at the last supper. None of these things would have occurred in the kingly scenario.

Because Jesus was a free agent, he met many people on the roadside. When people met him on the road, they asked questions. We would not have many of the 300 subjects Jesus taught, unless Jesus had left heavens precincts to come and live among ordinary people so that they could ask him these questions.

These answers are among the most treasured teachings of Jesus. Some of the parables he told were only told because people he met asked him questions. The parable of the good Samaritan is one such example. Another example are these words.

> "God is seeking worshipers who worship him in spirit and in truth."

These are the words he spoke to a Samaritan woman at a Jacob's well, after he struck up a conversation with her. Jesus would never have gone to her village if he had to abide by an official program and she would never have got near him, if the religious authorities had been controlling the program as in the king of King scenario.

Another example of treasured teachings was the result of being questioned on the street.

> "The two greatest commandments are these. "Love the Lord Your God with all your heart mind and soul. And the second is like it. Love your neighbor as yourself" Matt 22:28

Other treasured teachings we have are in response to teachers of the law who met him on the streets and were trying to trap him.

> "Render to Caesar, that which is Caesars, and to God, that which is God's."

Then there are many stories in the Gospels

we would not have if Jesus had come as a glorious king. We would not have for example Jesus words to Peter, said three times after His resurrection. "Do you love me.....?" This was an example of, gracious forgiveness. This example of gracious forgiveness would not have occurred if Jesus had come as a glorious king as in the king of Kings scenario..

> (a) Because Jesus would never have been crucified and
> (b) Peter, being a Galilean fisherman, is unlikely to have been allowed near King Jesus.

*All crucifixions were canceled during the glorious king scenario.

This example with Peter and other acts of grace would never have occurred if Jesus had come as a glorious King.

It was while on the road Jesus heard about a centurions servant who was very sick. And on the road, he heard about the daughter of a synagogue ruler who was near death. On the road, he met the father of a boy with a demon, which kept trying to harm him. While traveling, lepers approached him. These people would never have got near him in the glorious King scenario, for troops and security personnel would have kept them at bey.

During his itinerant ministry, Jesus talked face to face with many people over dinner tables. Mary and Martha, the twelve disciples, Zaachaeus, a Pharisee.

Jesus would not have known suffering and betrayal if he had come as a glorious king. He never would have forgiven the condemned criminal on a nearby cross. He never would have died for our sins, and risen, victorious over death.

Some Christians today almost overdo the humble circumstance of Jesus birth. It was humble but at the same time, there was a mosaic of witnesses to the birth of the Son of God. From the heavenly realm, an army of angels. From the cosmos, a bright star. From the animal world, cattle and sheep? From the working classes, shepherds. From the realm of the powerful, three highly ranked Government advisors (wise men). All of these formed a godly mosaic of witnesses to his birth as the Son of God.

The timing of his birth, was perfect. The place of his birth was perfect – and the way he came (as the son of Mary) was perfect. Perfect for what God planned for him and perfect for Jesus to achieve among the people of his time what God planned - and all because he came as the Son of God - incarnate in a human body.

Chapter 5

The Purposes of the Incarnation

When the pilot of a commercial airliner turns up at an airport, he or she is not there, merely to visit the shops. The pilot is there for a particular purpose. That purpose is to co-operate with all the other airline staff and employees of other organizations such as air traffic controllers, re-fuelers and baggage handlers for the same purpose. To ensure paid passengers arrive safely at their destination. The pilot's job is finished once all of the passengers have disembarked safely from his aircraft.

When Jesus came to this earth he did not come for a sight-seeing visit. He came with a mission to complete. A mission planned in agreement with his Father prior to the start of that mission. He knew the mission was complete when on the cross he cried "it is finished".

There is a sense in which his mission becomes even more complete when each disciple finishes their own mission on Earth, and Jesus says to them

> "Well done, good and faithful servant....Matt 25:21

For that was part of the of the overall plan, to create disciples from all nations. These disciples would be witnesses in Judea, Samaria and the ends of the Earth. In this, Jesus instructed his disciples to reach every person living on Earth. This is approached on a gradient, firstly with family, friends, colleagues, and then strangers in ones community, eventually extending to other communities and other nations.

Unlike an airline Captain who has one single purpose, Jesus had a number of purposes to fulfill when he came incarnate to this earth in human form.

His coming was purpose-laden! From Jesus' own words we can see that he entered earth's precincts, knowing exactly what those purposes were.

- "For even the Son of Man did not come to be served, he came to serve and give his life to redeem many people."Mark 10:45 (G.N)
- "For the Son of Man came to seek and save what was lost."Luke 19:10 (NIV)
- "For I have not come to call the righteous, but sinners." Matt 9:13 (NIV)
- "The thief comes only to steal and kill and destroy; I have come that they might have life, and have it to the full." John 10:10 (NIV)

You will notice in each of these verses, Jesus repeats the same message, "I have come..." These were some of the key reasons Jesus came.

By reviewing Jesus ministry, it is possible to see many other reasons for his coming and it is reasonable to assume that these 'other purposes' were discussed in the heavenly council before he came.

- He came to communicate God's truth.
- He came to show (demonstrate) the love of God.
- He came to set people free from all

sorts of bondages. From demons, money, power, and false religions.
- He came to call people to be his disciples, and establish the Church.

PURPOSE ONE – he came to communicate God's truth – direct from heaven

Jesus, when praying for his disciples, said these words.

> "For everything that I learned from my Father I have made known to you." John 15:15 (NIV)

There was a widespread expectation that the Messiah, when he came, would tell God's people everything! We find that expectation on the lips of the Samaritan woman Jesus talked to, at a well. She said.

> "I know that the Messiah is coming. When he comes, he will explain **everything** to us." John 4:25 (emphasis added)

Jesus confirmed what the Samaritan woman expected of the Messiah. When speaking to the twelve disciples not long before he left this earth, he said to them

> "**everything** I have learned from my Father, I have made known to

you." John 15:15(emphasis added)

The writer of the book of Hebrews underlined the distinction between the great prophets like Moses, and Jesus.

> "In the past days God spoke to our ancestors many times and in many ways through the prophets, but in these last days he has spoken to us through his Son." Heb 1:1-2a (G.N)

That was one of the key reasons God finally decided to send his Son, incarnate, into our world.

Before Jesus came to this earth, there had been many wonderful men and women of God. Some, like Moses, actually talked with God. Marvelous though that was, Moses gained only a limited insight of his God. Jesus by contrast had been speaking with God from before the world was created. He described himself...

> "... a man who has told you the truth that I heard from God." John 8:40 (NIV)

At least five subjects convey Jesus' unique knowledge - a knowledge no prophet had. A knowledge that could only come from someone who had come from heaven, and been in the presence of God.

HEAVEN

(1) A knowledge of the nature of heaven. While hanging on the cross he told the repentant criminal

> "I tell you the truth, today you will
>
> be with me in paradise." Luke 23:43 (NIV)

Jesus was confident about where he was going and where this repentant criminal was going also - paradise. He was able to describe what is in heaven. He told the first disciples

> "There are many rooms in my Father's house.... John 14:2 (G.N)

Those words suggest that he had been inside those rooms. Other conversations Jesus had, indicates his unique knowledge of heaven. He told the Sadducee's that there is no marriage in heaven, but that we will have bodies like angels. Matt 22:30

(2) Because Jesus came from heaven, he was able to make comparisons between heaven and earth. For example, he said

> "Do not store up for yourselves treasures on earth, where moth

> and rust destroy, where thieves
> break in and steal. But store up for
> yourselves treasures in heaven,
> where moth and rust do not
> destroy, and where thieves do not
> break in and steal." Matt 6:19-20
> (NIV)

Jesus was making the point that this earth is an unfavorable place to store treasures while heaven is a good place.

(3) Jesus was able to tell us that some things applied in both realms. He said

> "... whatever you bind on earth will
> be bound in heaven, and whatever
> you loose on earth will be loosed in
> heaven." Matt 16:19 (NIV)

(4) A unique knowledge of beings who live in heaven. God, the Holy Spirit, angels.

(i)   GOD, THE FATHER

John wrote

> "No one has ever seen God. The
> only son who is the same as God
> and is at the Father's side, he has
> made him known." John 1:18 (G.N)

Moses spoke with God, but God would not allow Moses to see his face, only his glory. However, Jesus who lived in the presence of

God was able to teach with authority those things that he knew about the nature of God. For example, he was able to tell the crowds listening to him on the hill-sides of Galilee

> "Your Father in heaven knows that you need all these things." Matt 6:32 (G.N)

It is implicit in Jesus' words that he 'knew' the Father intimately, to be able to confidently use the word "knows".

In the same teaching session, he said

> "You have heard that it was said, Love your neighbor and hate your enemy. But I tell you: Love your enemies and pray for those who persecute you, that you may be sons of your Father in heaven." Matt 5:43-44 (NIV)

Until mid way through the 20th century, it was common for the male form such as sons or his to include the female form daughters or her in written works. Other versions use the word "like", instead of sons.

During another teaching session Jesus indicated that he 'knew' God's heart towards those who ask.

> "How much more, then, will your

> Father in heaven give good things
> to those who ask him!" Matt 7:11
> (G.N)

All through his teachings are   examples of
Jesus' knowledge of God's nature.

(ii)   HOLY SPIRIT

The most common name for the Holy Spirit in
the Old Testament, was

> "The Spirit of the Lord... 1 Sam
> 10:6

Those listening to Jesus would have
immediately noticed that He never used those
words. He always referred to Him as either
"The Holy Spirit" or "Holy Spirit"*. Obviously
indicating that one of the most significant
attributes about the Spirit of the Lord, is that
he is holy!

> *In the original (Greek version) of the
> New Testament – Jesus often refers to
> the Holy Spirit as simply, "Holy Spirit".

Both terms, "The Holy Spirit" and "Holy Spirit",
imply that the 'The Spirit' is a personal being –
not just a divine force. This is confirmed by
another word Jesus used. Jesus used the
personal pronoun "He" when talking of the
Holy Spirit. Further, Jesus spoke of personal
roles that the Holy Spirit would assume such

as, being like a teacher and guide. John 16:13

(iii)   ANGELS

Every Jewish adult would have a basic knowledge of angels because they are mentioned throughout the Torah (The first five books), the Psalms and the Prophets. Jesus began to tell those who listened to him, additional characteristics of angels. For example, he was able to tell the Sadducee's that angels do not marry. Matt 22:30.

On another occasion, Jesus said angels rejoice over one sinner who repents. Mark 12:25 Jesus also told a story about an angel escorting a beggar into heaven and how at the end of the age, they will separate the wicked and the righteous. Mark 13:49-50

End of the Age

(5) In the book of Daniel and other prophets, there is limited information about the end of the age. Jesus, who came from heaven, predicted the destruction of Jerusalem in AD70, but also described the end of the age in greater detail – see Matthew chapter 24.

In summary, one of the purposes Jesus came to this earth was to tell the first disciples, (and by implication, we who follow in their footsteps) what only the 'Son' of God could know. From this brief survey, we can see that Jesus had a knowledge of heaven, of God the Father, of the Holy Spirit, of angels and of the end of the age, that only someone close to the Father would know. It was as the Samaritan woman (at the well) said

> "I know that the Messiah is coming. When he comes, he will **explain everything to us**." John 4:25 (emphasis added)

PURPOSE TWO – he came to show or demonstrate.

If purpose one was to 'tell', purpose two was to demonstrate or to set an example for the disciples who would follow after the first twelve. Because Jesus was in an essence, God (Phil 2:6), we can see in Jesus words and actions, God himself speaking and acting. Paul wrote to the Church at Colosse

> "He (Jesus) is the image of the invisible God." Col 1:15 (N.I.V)

And Jesus said himself,

> "Anyone who has seen me has seen the Father."John 14:9 (N.I.V)

C.S. Lewis wrote.

> In the same way the Church exists

> for nothing else but to draw men to Christ, to make them little Christs. If they are not doing that, all the Cathedrals, clergy, missions, sermons, even the Bible itself, is simply a waste of time. God became a man for no other purpose.
>
> C.S Lewis (A Year With C.S Lewis p158 – Harper San Francisco)

The old Apostle John had plenty of time to reflect on what made Jesus different from the religious leaders of his time, and even the prophets of old. He made this distinction

> "For the law was given through Moses; grace and truth came through Jesus Christ." John 1:17 (NIV)

Jesus was a demonstration of God's grace and truth. We can see how Jesus combined both "grace and truth" in the way he acted towards a woman caught in act of adultery. The teachers of the law brought her to Jesus, and threw her on the ground in front of him. The teachers of the law reminded Jesus, that according to the law, this woman should be stoned.

If Jesus had not been gracious he would have looked at her in disgust and agreed that she be stoned. Instead, Jesus stooped down and began to write in the sand, as if he had all the time in the world. After a pause, he said to the teachers of the law. "If anyone of you is without sin, let him be the first to throw a stone at her,"

Grace allows for the fact that we all are sinful, and Jesus after acting graciously towards her, then spoke graciously to her. He said,"Then neither do I condemn you..." After that, Jesus spoke words of truth

> "Go now and leave your life of sin."John 8:11

The reason Jesus told her to leave her life of sin (the truth) is he wanted her to be free. Jesus recognized that those who dismiss moral laws 'think' they are free. In fact they become slaves to sin.

> "Jesus replied, I tell you the truth, everyone who sins is a slave to sin." John 8:34 (NIV)

So a reason for Jesus' coming is that he as God's Son, was able to model both aspects of the nature of God. God's grace and God's truth.

All through his life we can see Jesus modeling the nature of God. Or put another way, God's signature could be seen in every action of Jesus, and heard in every word he spoke.

PURPOSE THREE – He came to destroy the works of the devil

Another purpose for Jesus coming was to destroy the works of the devil. 1 John 3:8

He did this in three ways.

- By delivering people from the power of Satan
- By giving the disciples authority over demons. Math 10:1
- By teaching the disciples about Satan and the activity of demons.

PURPOSE FOUR – He came to establish the Church

We know that the Church today has about 1.8 billion Christians in it, but it's starting point was the ministry of Jesus. The first disciples would not have recognized that purpose when Jesus first called them. Jesus was intent on establishing his Church through them. It is much easier to see this with the benefit of hindsight. When he first called the disciples, the first words to the fishermen were

"come follow me," and "I will make

you fishers of men." Matt 4:19

The disciples would become actively involved in fishing for (gathering) new disciples after Jesus ascended into heaven. Sometimes they came one by one, other times in their thousands. C.f. Acts 4:4

During the next three years, it is unlikely the first disciples would have recognized that Jesus was preparing them for their role as leaders of the new Church. We can see that preparation from what he taught them and what he got them to do.

- By sending them out on a mission trip. Matt 10:5-15
- Through teaching sessions E.g. John chapters 14-16
- Teaching them to pray. Luke 11:1-4 & Math 18:19-20
- To care for one another. John 13:5
- He showed them how to love people, the Pharisees called sinners - and to love people of other races. John 4:1-14
- To take Holy Communion to remember him. Matt 26:26-30
- To understand his style of servant leadership. Matt 20:25-27

Towards the end of his time with them, Jesus asked the disciples "Who do you say i am?" Peter's reply was, "You are the Christ, the Son of the living God." Jesus told Peter that God had revealed this to him, and then said

> "And I tell you that you are Peter, and on this rock I will build my Church....Matt 16:16-18

At that time, it is unlikely that Peter and the other disciples would have fully grasped what he meant. It would only be after he had returned to heaven, they would look back and say to themselves "Remember when Jesus was with us, He told us that the confession, "You are the Christ" will be the basis, on which we are to "build the Church."

When we look at his ministry, we can see the way Jesus prepared the disciples for the time when they would be leaders in the new Church.

After Jesus had risen from the dead he intensified that purpose. He told them

> "Therefore go and make disciples of all nations... Matt 28:19

and also

> "But you will receive power when the Holy Spirit comes on you, and you will be my witnesses in Jerusalem, and in all Judea and Samaria, and to the ends of the

earth." Acts 1:8

These words were like the icing on the cake. The cake that he began to prepare when He first called them and told them that they would become fishers of men.

PURPOSE FIVE – He Came to save the world

The name Jesus is the Greek form of the Hebrew word Joshua. Joshua is a contraction of the word "Jehoshua", meaning "Jehovah the Saviour" The name Jesus/Joshua is built on the Hebrew verb stem *yasha* meaning, saved. So when the angel instructed Mary to

name her son Jesus, it was an affirmation that he was to become 'the savior".

When we look at the birth, life, death and resurrection of Jesus, we can say "His life and death were salvation history". Two verses in particular, emphasize this point.

> "For God did not send his Son into the world to condemn the world, but to save the world through him." John 3:17

This is good and pleases God our Saviour, for he longs for all to be saved and to understand this truth.

> "That God is on one side and all the people on the other side, and Christ Jesus, himself man is between them to bring them together by giving his life for all mankind." 1 Tim 2:4-6 (L.B.)

In both verses can you see the word 'God' and the words 'save' or 'saved.' That was one of the key reasons Jesus came. God wanted to establish a new covenant with a new covenant people. People who would believe that Jesus died in their place for their sins so that they might be reconciled with God and made part of his family. A well known Christmas carol also emphasizes these points about why Jesus came.

> Hark, the herald angels sing,
> Glory to the new-born king
> Born that man no more may die
> Born to raise the sons of earth...

So the coming of Jesus, incarnate into our world, was purpose-laden! He came to tell us (what only the Son of God could know). He came to show or demonstrate God's way. He came to destroy the works of the devil. He came to establish the Church, to save us self-centered, sinful people and reconcile us with God the Father.

Chapter 6

What Does The Incarnation Mean To Us Today?

The coming of Jesus to this earth was purpose-laden. He came to tell us what only the Son of God could know. He came to show us God's way. He came to destroy the works of the devil. He came to establish his Church. He came to save us and reconcile us with God the Father.

I tried to convey in the chapter *Perfect Timing, Perfect Place* that Jesus coming as a glorious

king would have done limited good and
produced many many unwelcome side-
effects. Then there were other possibilities.
God could have decided to skip the glorious
king scenario and just written the words of
Jesus on the clouds, but would people of that
time have taken notice of messages written in
the sky?

It is likely that the people of two thousand
years ago and the people of today, would
have treated words written on the clouds as a
novelty. Something to be talked about, then
forgotten.

People of that time took notice because God's
word to us came in the form of a human
being. It is because Jesus came to this Earth
and lived what he taught, is what makes
following Jesus, so appealing. Having Jesus
as the living word, is a world of difference to
having God merely writing his words in the
clouds.

The significance of Jesus coming to this Earth
to share our human existence was highlighted
by an experience I had over a decade ago,
when my daughter was around 12 or 13yrs
old. At that time she, along with other
members of her youth group decided to do the

World Vision 40 hour fast. As we began to talk over the details of what it would mean for her, I suggested that it would become a "real struggle" towards the end of the fast, so I began to wonder.

How could I possibly encourage her to keep going towards the end of the 40 hours, when her stomach is grumbling and she is looking longingly at all the food we are eating (breakfast, lunch and dinner, not to mention the snacks in between), and at the same time; to encourage her to keep going, when I had a full stomach?

In the end I decided the only way I could encourage a hungry daughter to keep going, was to be doing the exactly same thing she was doing, fasting!

As expected, when our bodies began to miss those regular snacks and meals they were used to, our stomachs began to grumble. Between about twenty and thirty hours after the fast began, my daughter and I exchanged comments, like. "How 'good' the food on the table, looks." About thirty hours after the start of the fast, my daughter turned to me and said with some anguish.

"Dad, I'm so hungry!" Without thinking about my response, I said with the same anguish, "I know!"

It is those words, "I know" that encapsulates the significance of the incarnation. Jesus, the Son of God can say to us "I know!" about virtually every human experience we go through because He has been there. Laughter and tears. Tedious* jobs and exhilarating jobs. Health and pain. Love and rejection. A Lord and Saviour who stayed in heaven would not be able to say those words, "I know."

> *I thought about Jesus doing tedious jobs while I was sweeping leaves out of the garage one day – and the thought occurred to me at that time, that Jesus must have swept wood chips from his carpenters shop each day.

The old Apostle John, aware that some were saying Jesus was more like a spirit being, affirmed Jesus was both the Son of God and at the same time, a normal human being. He wrote

> "The Word became a **human being** and, full of grace and truth, lived among us." John 1:14 (GN – emphasis added)

The author of the book of Hebrews wrote the same thing, using different words:

"For we do not have a high priest who is unable to sympathize with our weaknesses, but we have one who has been tempted in every way, just as we are - yet without sin. Let us then approach the throne of grace with confidence, so that we may receive mercy and find grace to help us in our time of need. Heb 4:15-16 (NIV)

The words 'lived among us' are a reminder that he was born in a manger and raised in an ordinary home, rather than in a palace, or in the home of a priestly family, a fact that would have allowed him to serve in the Temple. The words living among us meant he grew up sharing a normal life and doing things like receiving an education, playing with other children, being hurt and teased.

Living in a normal home where his brothers and sisters would have had normal disagreements over what was fair and what was right. A normal human life meant that as he grew older he would begin working, rather than going to one of the religious schools and becoming either a Pharisee, Sadducee or Priest.

Because he became "a human being", during his time on Earth he would fully share our humanity, meaning that at times he would become hungry, tired and even angry.

Humbling himself and choosing to lead a normal human life meant leaving the door open to enduring a number of human frailties. Being misunderstood by people. Being misrepresented by people. The Pharisees said he had a demon. Being lied about. Being denied by friends (Peter), and even betrayed by friends (Judas).

On the flip-side it meant that he would experience normal pleasures as well. Celebrating happy occasions like weddings. Celebrating the birth of children to his sister-in-laws. Taking children in his arms to bless them. Seeing the joy on the face of the leper when he was healed. Seeing the amazement on the face of the ruler of the Synagogue when his daughter was healed.

Other normal pleasures Jesus would have enjoyed because he became a human like us included enjoying food. Enjoying sunshine, or picking corn as he strolled through the fields. Satisfaction at the end of a day's work. Seeing his disciples advance in their readiness to be leaders. Enjoying sights such as, hillsides full of lilies.

Because Jesus shared our humanity and understands human experience, this ought to frame our prayer life.

The way Jesus came incarnate from heaven into our world as a normal human being, is also the model for our Christian life. Jesus came incarnate into our World and asked his disciples to go incarnate into their World. He came as a light, and wants us to be a light.

We disciples of Jesus are also encouraged to go incarnate into our world. Meaning people in our immediate neighborhood, our families, those we work and study with. Incarnate into pre-schools, schools and institutions of higher learning.

Incarnate into the world of sports and culture, music and entertainment. Incarnate into the worlds of both success and failure, riches and poverty.

Incarnate into the media or mines, factories or farms. I.T. or transport. Medicine or manufacturing, science or sales, the stock exchange or slums. Fishing or forestry, politics or tourism, manufacturing or engineering. Wholesale or retail. A Government employee, or self employed. Peace corps or the military.

Whatever people do. Wherever people are,

120   What Does The Incarnation Mean To Us Today?

Jesus wants his disciples to be incarnate in every corner of society, in the same way he came incarnate into our world.

Chapter 7

Love God

I wrote in the introduction that this book is as much about the nature of God, as it is about Jesus coming incarnate into our world. When Jesus came, it was as if, God had sent us a present. That present came, wrapped in baby's clothes and had there been a card it may have read:

TO THE HUMAN RACE

THIS IS EMMANUEL*

Love
God

*meaning God with us.

Appendix

The purpose of a creed is to provide a doctrinal statement of correct belief, or orthodoxy.

The creeds of Christianity have been drawn up at times of conflict about doctrine: acceptance or rejection of a creed served to distinguish believers and deniers of a particular doctrine or set of doctrines.

The original Nicene Creed was first adopted in the year 325AD at the First Council of Nicaea. At that time, the text ended after the words "we believe in the Holy Spirit."

The Nicene Creed reproduced here is the original creed, as adopted in 325AD at the First Council of Nicaea.

- <u>Wikipedia</u>

The Nicene Creed

We believe in one God, the Father Almighty, Maker of all things visible and invisible.

And in one Lord Jesus Christ, the Son of God, begotten of the Father the only-begotten, that is, of the essence of the Father, God of God, Light of Light, very God of very God, begotten, not made, being of one substance with the Father,

By whom all things were made both in heaven and on earth,

Who for us men, and for our salvation, came down and was incarnate and was made man,

He suffered, and the third day he rose again, ascended into heaven,

From thence he shall come to judge the quick and the dead.

And we believe in the Holy Spirit.